SCHOOL LIBRARY SERVICE

James		
Neil		
Warren		
Warren		
Andrew K.		

SPACE LIBRARY
SPACESHIPS
GREGORY VOGT

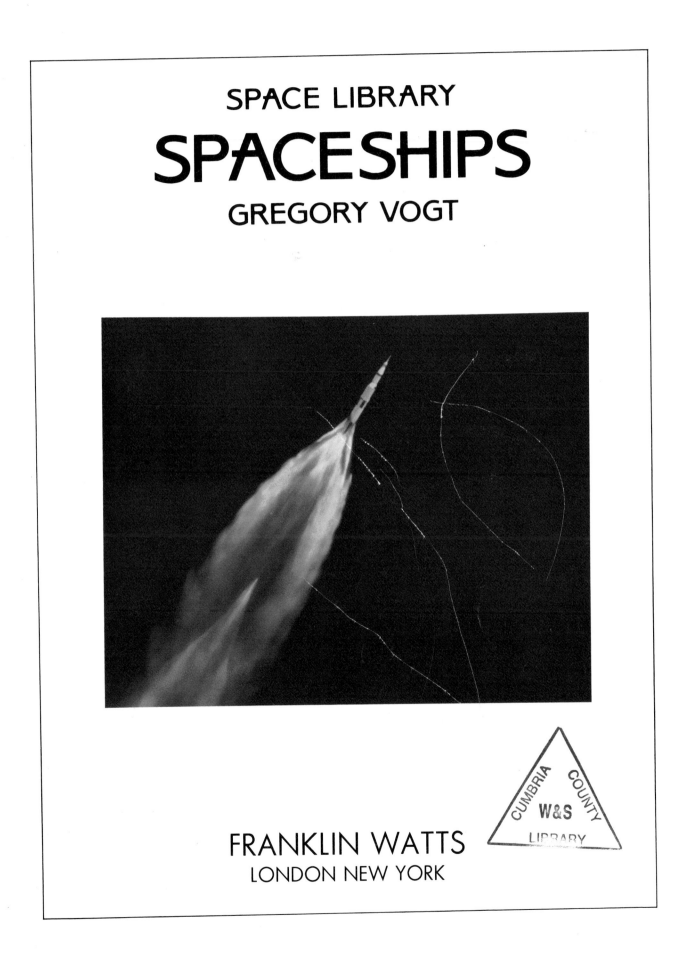

FRANKLIN WATTS
LONDON NEW YORK

Each new generation of humankind has had the challenge of a frontier. The frontier for today's children is outer space; it beckons with unlimited experiences. It is the frontier of my children, and I dedicate this book to them.

Kirsten, Allison and Catherine Vogt

First published in the USA
by Franklin Watts Inc.
387 Park Ave. South
New York, N.Y. 10016

First published in Great Britain in 1990 by
Franklin Watts
96 Leonard Street
London EC2A 4RH

First published in Australia
by Franklin Watts
Australia
14 Mars Road
Lane Cove, NSW 2066

US ISBN: 0-531-10405-2
UK ISBN: 0 86313 5994
Library of Congress
Catalog Card No: 87-50169

Designed by Michael Cooper

All photographs courtesy of NASA except: Movie Star News: p. 6;
The Granger Collection: p. 7 (top left and right); ESA: pp. 8
(bottom right), 9 (both), 24, 25 (both); Tass from Sovfoto:
pp. 10, 11 (top left and right); British Aerospace Co.: p. 27.

CONTENTS

ASTRONAUTS ALL

In classrooms around the world teachers often ask students 'What do you want to be when you grow up?' Although there are many answers, one seems to come up often. Perhaps it is your answer: 'I want to be an astronaut.' Being an astronaut is one of the most exciting professions to consider. Whether you realise it or not, you don't have to wait to grow up to be an astronaut. You are one already. From the moment you were born, you have been on a voyage through space. If you are ten years old, you have already travelled nearly 9 billion, 700 million kilometres (6 billion miles) through space. If you live to be 100 years old, you will have travelled one one-hundredth the distance of a light year without even setting foot off Earth. (A light year is the distance that light travels in one year. It is about the same as 9 and one-half million million kilometres or six million million miles.)

How, you wonder, is such a space journey possible when you have spent your entire life on the surface of Earth? It is possible if you don't look at Earth merely as a wide expanse of land and water, but as a planet orbiting the Sun. Day and night, month after month, year after year, Earth is on a journey. It orbits our Sun at the rate of 108,000 km/h (67,000 mph). Each orbit of the Sun is nearly one billion kilometres (about 600 million miles) in length.

As creatures of Earth, we accompany the planet on its space journey. That makes us astronauts. The Earth is our spaceship and it is well equipped for our journey. Its motion around the Sun is our propulsion system.

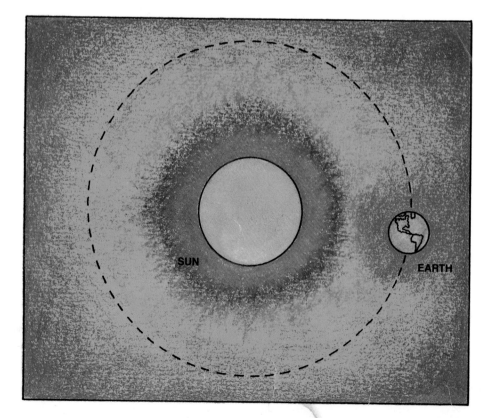

There are only two significant things about spaceship Earth that make it different from the mechanical spaceships that send astronauts into orbit or towards the Moon. One is that we astronauts live and function on the outside of our spaceship under a blanket of air that is held in place by Earth's gravitational field. The second and really important difference is that we go wherever our spaceship goes. We have no control over our journey. Earth travels on a course set at the creation of our Solar System.

The other kind of spaceship is a sealed container that keeps astronauts and atmosphere inside. Mechanical spaceships are controlled by the astronauts inside and are able to change speed and direction. Travelling in a mechanical spaceship is what you were really thinking about when you thought about being an astronaut. Spaceships are just an extension of an age-old dream of flight that has fascinated humans for thousands of years.

(Left) In 1972 Apollo 17 took this picture of spaceship Earth from a distance of 160,000 km (100,000 mi). (Above) In 1968 three Apollo astronauts looked back at Earth while they were orbiting the Moon. The view showed them how solitary it looked and how important it is to preserve our planet.

Barely visible as a thin bluish line covering the curved surface of the Earth over the Strait of Gibraltar, the atmosphere makes life on the surface of spaceship Earth possible.

AN ANCIENT INVENTION

'Mr Scott. Warp factor two.' On many an exciting mission, Captain James T. Kirk of the Starship *Enterprise* orders his chief engineer, Mr Scott, to power up the matter/antimatter engines for a faster-than-light trip through the galaxy. Stars go whizzing by and distances that would take spaceship Earth millions of years are travelled in only a few hours. Science fiction is exciting, but we have to remember it is only what it says it is: fiction. Matter/antimatter engines are a fantasy that may become real in the future. What is true now is that there are spaceships capable of carrying people off the surface of Earth into space. Though their speeds seem like a snail's pace compared to those in films, they do work. And they are, for the moment, the only way we have of venturing off Planet Earth.

Although spaceships have been around for only the past twenty-five years or so, they owe their existence to some really ancient inventions. One was an important discovery made nineteen hundred years ago, that a mixture of three chemicals—sulphur, charcoal and saltpetre—would explode when burned. The mixture was called black powder. After many hundreds of years of experimentation, someone succeeded in producing an arrow that flew through the air by the force of this burning powder. It was the invention of the rocket. No one knows for sure who invented the rocket, but it was most likely someone who lived nine hundred years ago in China.

The rocket was the start of space travel. Though the Space Shuttle is much bigger, more powerful and more complex, the principles behind its flight are not very different from those that governed the flight of the ancient Chinese fire arrows. It was Isaac Newton who explained it all.

'Warping' through the universe, the Starship *Enterprise* carries the crew of the popular TV show 'Star Trek' to amazing adventures.

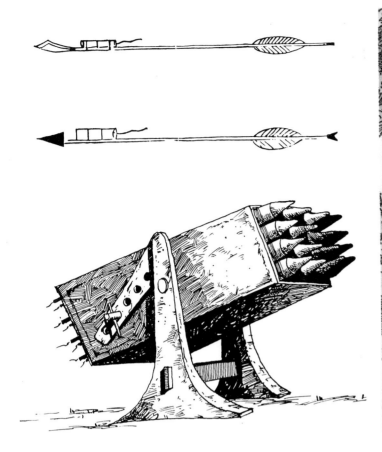

Newton was a famous English scientist who lived between 1642 and 1727. Among his many accomplishments, Newton discovered the law of gravity, explained how satellites could be orbited above Earth and outlined the principles of rocketry. These principles are known today as Newton's Three Laws of Motion.

The first law is an obvious statement of fact, but one that has enormous implications for space flight. Newton pointed out that an object that is not moving will stay that way unless it is acted upon by a force. He also stated that if an object is moving, it will keep on moving unless it is acted upon by a force. What this means to rocketry is that a spaceship in space doesn't need to keep firing its engines to keep moving. Unlike a car, which is continually being slowed by friction with the road and the air, a spaceship can travel at fantastic speeds for billions of kilometres just by coasting. The purpose of a spaceship's rocket engine is to speed up or slow down the spaceship or change its direction.

In the second law, Newton stated that force is equal to two things that are multiplied together. When applied to rocket engines, one is the mass or amount of rocket exhaust (burning gases escaping through the engine) and the other is how fast it escapes. In the third law, Newton stated that every action has an opposite and equal reaction. You have probably felt this yourself many times. An especially embarrassing and wet opportunity comes when someone tries to step off a boat onto a pier without first tying up the boat.

Notice, in these three laws, that nowhere does Newton say a rocket engine pushes on the air outside it. This is a mistaken idea about rockets. If it were true, rockets wouldn't work in space because there isn't any air there.

(Left) The roots of modern rocketry go back to the Chinese 'fire arrows' of the 11th century. Early rocketeers quickly discovered the rocket's use for warfare. In the 13th century, Mongolian invaders used clusters of rockets mounted in boxes to fire on enemy defences.
(Above) Sir Isaac Newton contemplates the laws of gravity and motion while resting under an apple tree.

EXPLOSIONS AND LIFT-OFFS

In the first years of the space age, the riskiest part of space flight was getting there. The first unmanned rockets were unreliable. At the moment of lift-off, many just sat on the launch pad. Some tilted, fell over and blew up. Some rose majestically, started tumbling and blew up, while others just sat there and blew up. There were many reasons for failure, but the primary cause is that the surface of Earth is at the bottom of a great gravity well. Climbing out of the well to outer space takes a tremendous amount of energy. A rocket is the only way to do it. Unfortunately rockets are very heavy. Most of their weight is not found in the nose cone or the engines or the metal walls. About 90 percent of the weight is in fuel for the journey. At the moment of lift-off, much of the energy of the engine's thrust is used just to raise fuel into the air that will be needed later.

Today, about thirty years since the first successful satellite launch, many nations have used reliable space rockets. The United States has its Space Shuttle, Delta, Atlas, Scout and Titan rockets. The Soviet Union has a space fleet of more than half a dozen rockets of different sizes to carry payloads of different weights and destinations. Japan, China and India also have space rockets.

(Left) Dr Robert Goddard began the age of modern rocketry with his experiments with liquid propellants. He stands beside the world's first successful liquid-fuel rocket before it lifted off on 16 March 1926.
(Below) An Ariane 3 rocket lifts off with two satellites on board on 4 August 1984.

Ariane launch site in French Guiana.

An ejection test of the fairing, or nose cone, for an Ariane rocket. During the test, conducted in a vacuum chamber to simulate the space environment, the fairing opened almost like a clamshell.

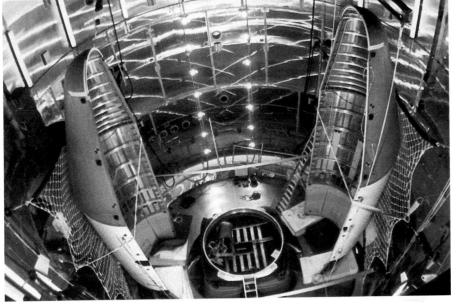

In Western Europe, no one nation has a rocket of its own. Instead, a group of nations have joined together to form the European Space Agency (ESA) to build Ariane. Ariane is actually a family of rockets. Ariane 3 and 4 are currently being used by ESA for unmanned payloads. Ariane 5, planned for the future, will be able to carry unmanned or manned payloads.

Like most modern space rockets, the Arianes are multistaged. Each has three stages, although the higher numbered Arianes also have several small strap-on solid or liquid rocket boosters to provide additional lift-off thrust. The first two stages of Ariane use hypergolic propellants. Hypergolic means that the propellants burn when they make contact with each other. Various mixtures of exotic-sounding chemicals such as nitrogen tetroxide and unsymmetrical dimethylhydrazine are used. The third stage uses liquid hydrogen and liquid oxygen.

With Ariane, the European Space Agency has gone into the business of launching satellites. They not only launch their own payloads, but they compete with the Space Shuttle for the launching of communications satellites of other nations.

ANIMALS LEAD THE WAY

'Spam in the can' is what envious US Air Force test pilots called the seven astronauts chosen for the Mercury space programme in 1958. The seven were to be strapped into a tiny cone-shaped 'bucket of bolts' and blasted into space. For all the benefit the astronauts were to be to the mission, it was said, they might as well send up chimpanzees instead. You can imagine the pilots' delight when that is exactly what happened.

Both the United States and the Soviet Union were eager to be the first to launch humans into space. However, no one knew whether humans could survive the launch itself let alone flying around in space. The safest way to answer this question was to send animals up first. The Soviets began on 3 November 1957 by launching a little dog named Kudryavka into orbit in Sputnik 2. Most people called the dog by its breed name, Laika. Laika survived the launch and lived several days in orbit until her oxygen ran out.

The United States chose to make its test flights with squirrel monkeys and later chimpanzees because these animals were more like humans than dogs were. Ham, the chimp, flew four years after Laika, on 31 January 1961. Ham's flight was suborbital, which means that it never reached orbit. On coming down, his rocket overshot the planned recovery zone in the Atlantic Ocean by more than 193 km (120 mi). The unhappy Ham sat in his capsule bobbing in the ocean for hours before recovery crews finally found him.

After launching several more satellites with dogs and bringing them safely back to Earth, the Soviets were confident they were ready to launch the first human into outer space. The honour for that flight fell to Russian cosmonaut Yuri A. Gagarin. On 12 April 1961, Gagarin, wearing a pressure suit, climbed inside a Vostok 1 space capsule. The Vostok spaceship was a cylinder 2.7 m (9 ft) in diameter and 5.1 m (17 ft) long. The nose-cone capsule in which Gagarin rode was a sphere that gave the entire spaceship a bulletlike appearance. After reaching space, Gagarin orbited Earth just once and returned. The sphere, with an outer layer of heat-protective material, safely re-entered the atmosphere. Before landing, Gagarin followed what would become standard practice for Vostok missions. A hatch opened at 6,900 m (23,000 ft) above Earth. At 3,900 m (13,000 ft) an ejection seat popped Gagarin out so that he and the spaceship landed by separate parachutes.

The Soviets launched five more Vostoks, including one carrying the first woman astronaut, Valentina Tereshkova. By October 1964, they were ready with a larger and heavier three-cosmonaut Voskhod spaceship. The 7.6 m (25 ft) long Voskhod provided room inside the capsule for the cosmonauts to release themselves from their seats and to float inside freely. A new braking system fired rocket blasts from the bottom of the capsule as parachutes brought it to within metres of the ground. The rockets cushioned their landing.

The dog Laika is about to be sealed into a container and placed on board Sputnik 2 for the first orbital test of a living creature.

After two planned flights of Voskhod, including one in which Alexei Leonov became the first space walker, a new Soviet spaceship, Soyuz, was introduced in April 1967. The capsule of this spaceship was larger still. It was sufficiently manoeuvrable to rendezvous and dock with Salyut space stations and with the American Apollo spaceship in 1975. The Soyuz was originally designed for three cosmonauts, but after an accident in which three cosmonauts died when a Soyuz lost pressure, only two people flew it.

Soyuz came in three pieces. The nose end was a sphere that served as an orbital space station for space experiments. Connected to it was a bell-shaped capsule with seats for the crew. The third part was a service module cylinder that contained radio, electric power, heat-control equipment and fuel for manoeuvring rocket engines.

(Left) Soviet Vostok spaceship on display. (Above) The cabin of the spaceship in which cosmonauts Pavel Belyayev and Alexei Leonov travelled in space in 1965.

NASA Apollo astronauts photographed the Soviet Soyuz spacecraft during the 1975 Apollo-Soyuz docking mission.

THE FIRST AMERICAN SHIPS

While the Soviets were perfecting their spaceships, American scientists were also working on their designs. NASA began its manned space mission on 5 May 1961 with the Mercury programme.

Alan Shepard was the first American to reach space. His flight lasted fifteen minutes before the Mercury capsule splashed down in the ocean, proving it was safe. As a safety measure, a red escape tower rocket was mounted on top of the black capsule to pull it away from the big rocket in an emergency.

Following a second suborbital flight, John Glenn became the first American to orbit Earth. As he rode in his capsule at 28,000 km/h (17,544 mph) he watched through a periscope as Earth passed beneath him. Early in the flight, ground controllers received a signal from the spaceship that its compressed-air landing bag was not locked in place. The bag was mounted underneath Mercury's heat shield and served to provide some cushioning on impact with the water. If the bag were loose, the heat shield might come off and Glenn would burn up on re-entry. It was decided that a retro rocket package, mounted beneath the shield and intended for slowing the capsule for re-entry, would be left in place after firing instead of being released as planned. Straps holding the package might also hold the heat shield. The plan worked and Glenn splashed down safely in the Atlantic. In the end, it was discovered that the landing bag signal had been a false alarm.

(Left) The Mercury space capsule in which Alan Shepard rode is hoisted on top of the Redstone booster rocket.
(Below) Alan Shepard begins his suborbital flight on board a Mercury Redstone rocket on 5 May 1961.

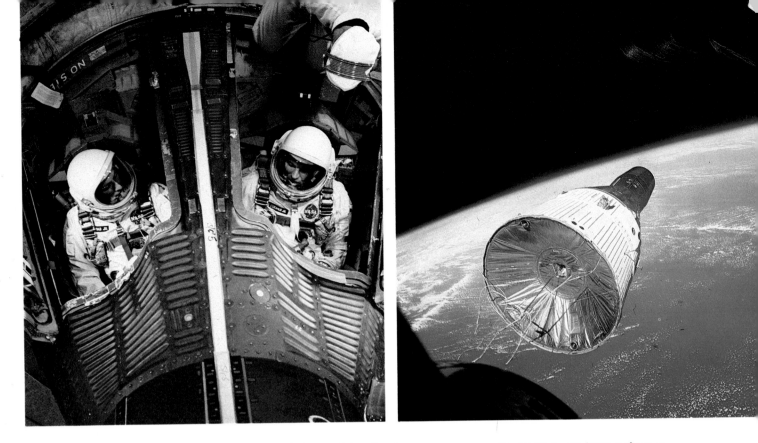

The six manned Mercury flights were followed by the two-astronaut Gemini programme. At 3.3 m high and 2.3 m wide (11 by 7½ ft), the craft was not much bigger than Mercury. Considering that two astronauts were inside, the fit was even tighter. Gemini 7 astronauts Frank Borman and Jim Lovell had to cope in their cramped quarters for fourteen days in orbit!

In addition to the capsule, Gemini also had a large adapter at its base that lengthened the spaceship by an extra 2.3 m (7½ ft). The adapter carried rockets, electric power and cooling equipment and was released before re-entry so that the blunt end of the capsule could survive the heat of friction with the air.

The Gemini programme had ten manned flights and it enabled the astronauts to try space walking and to practise rendezvous and docking techniques that would be necessary later with the Apollo trips to the Moon.

(Left) Though larger than a Mercury capsule, Gemini 5 astronauts Gordon Cooper and Charles Conrad find the capsule a snug fit.
(Above) The Gemini 7 space capsule was photographed by the crew of Gemini 6 during a rendezvous of the two capsules on 15 December 1965.

The prime crew of the first Apollo flight—Virgil Grissom (left), Roger Chaffee (centre) and Ed White (right). The three later died tragically in a capsule fire during a test.

13

SPACESHIP TO THE MOON

Imagine yourself riding on a wooden horse on a funfair roundabout. Hundreds of metres away, a golf ball is flying through the air. You raise a rifle to your shoulder and with one shot hit a mark on the moving ball. It is a very difficult task. Something similar, on a much grander scale, was achieved six times between 1969 and 1972 with project Apollo. A giant Saturn V rocket blasted off a rotating Earth and sent spaceship and astronauts more than 386,000 km (240,000 mi) across space to land on a moving Moon.

Everything about Apollo missions was big. The Saturn V rocket that began the journey was as tall as a 36-storey building: 109 m (363 ft). At lift-off, it had a mass of nearly 2,766,900 kg (6,100,000 lb). Five engines were required to provide the lift-off thrust.

At the top of the rocket, just below a white escape tower, was the capsule or command module. The cone-shaped capsule was 2.1 m high and 3 m in diameter (7 by 10 ft) and held three astronauts. Except during re-rentry, it was attached to a cylindrical service module containing electric power and cooling equipment like the adapter on Gemini. Furthermore, its large rocket engine provided the thrust to return home from the Moon.

In spite of its small size, the command module served as cockpit, bedroom, office, radio and TV studio, kitchen, bathroom, storage room for lunar samples and scientific laboratory. Apollo became NASA's 'workhorse' for eleven missions in the lunar programme, including six that landed. It also served in three Skylab flights in 1973 and 1974 and the Apollo-Soyuz mission in 1975.

The Saturn V rocket carrying the Apollo 11 crew to the Moon lifts off from NASA's launch complex 39A.

Apollo command and service modules orbiting above the lunar surface. This photograph was taken by the crew in the lander craft.

The lunar module with Neil Armstrong and Buzz Aldrin pulls away from the command module and prepares for the first manned landing on the Moon.

The first and second stages of Saturn V served only as boosters and never reached orbit. During the ascent, the third-stage engine fired and accelerated the crew and their spaceship to the Moon. Upon doing so, its job was finished. However, before parting with it, the astronauts manoeuvred their command and service module around and came back to the third stage nose-first in order to dock with the spiderlike lunar module. This was the spacecraft that would actually reach the Moon. The two-piece lander consisted of an ascent module as well as the descent module with its four unfolding legs and foot pads.

Upon reaching lunar orbit, two of the astronauts crawled through a tunnel into the lander and powered up its system. On cue, the craft separated from the command module and they began their descent by firing the powerful engine of the descent module. Spaced around the outside of the ascent module were four clusters of four small rockets. Small thrusts from these rockets enabled the lander to steer. Gradually, the main engine slowed the lander so that its legs touched down on the lunar soil.

Following sample collecting, setting up scientific experiments and exploring craters and lunar rills, it was time for the astronauts to leave the Moon. For lift-off, the descent module served as a launching platform and only the ascent module took off powered by the large engine at its base.

With careful space navigation, the lander crew and the third astronaut (who remained in the command module) docked and prepared to go home. After all samples were transferred to the command module, the lander was released and sent crashing back to the Moon. At this point the large service module rocket was activated and provided the push for the three-day return trip back to Earth.

Eventually this rocket too was jettisoned, leaving just the command module. The blunt heat shield glowed red hot as it re-entered the atmosphere and finally a small drogue parachute popped out to slow and stabilise the capsule. This was soon replaced by three much larger chutes that brought the capsule in for splashdown in the Pacific Ocean.

WINGED SPACESHIP

The seeds for space travel were sown during World War II. German rocket scientists were hard at work developing the V2 missile. Fortunately for the Allied nations—and in particular Great Britain—the V2 entered the war too late for its destructive potential to be realised. Though engaged in building weapons, the dream of some of those scientists was to build spaceships. One such scientist was Wernher von Braun who, following the war, emigrated to the United States to help pioneer its space programme.

In the early 1950s, von Braun and his colleagues described their vision of the first manned spaceship that would leave Earth. It was a long tapering cone 19.7 m (65 ft) in diameter at its base and as tall as a 24-storey office building. Fifty-one rockets in its base would consume 23.1 million kg (50.9 million lb) of nitric acid and hydrazine propellants in just 84 seconds. A second stage would fire, followed by the third. As the third stage continued its journey, the first and second stages would parachute back to Earth.

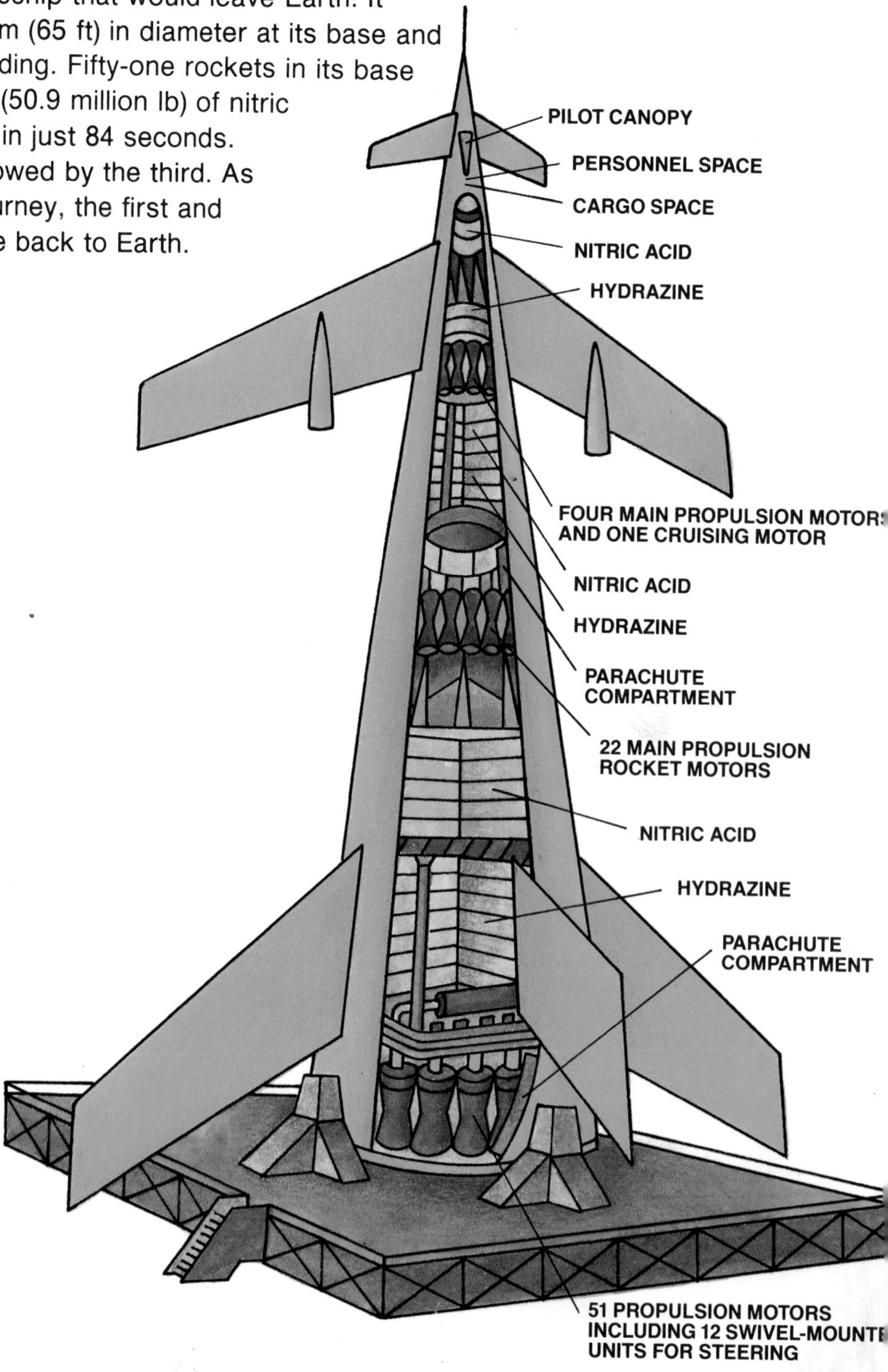

Wernher von Braun's concept of a winged spaceship in the 1950s was the forerunner of the Space Shuttle.

PILOT CANOPY

PERSONNEL SPACE

CARGO SPACE

NITRIC ACID

HYDRAZINE

FOUR MAIN PROPULSION MOTORS AND ONE CRUISING MOTOR

NITRIC ACID

HYDRAZINE

PARACHUTE COMPARTMENT

22 MAIN PROPULSION ROCKET MOTORS

NITRIC ACID

HYDRAZINE

PARACHUTE COMPARTMENT

51 PROPULSION MOTORS INCLUDING 12 SWIVEL-MOUNTED UNITS FOR STEERING

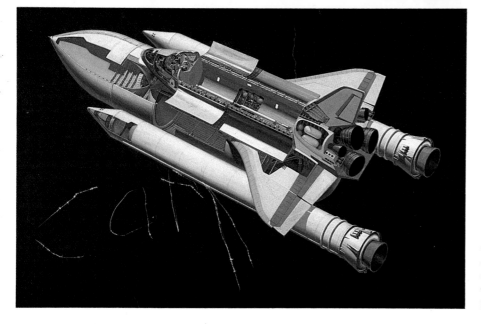

It was the third stage that made this rocket remarkable. It was a needle-shaped plane with wide swept-back wings and a crew compartment that held ten astronauts. After going into orbit and re-entry, the wings would enable the spaceship to glide safely back to Earth as a plane.

Von Braun's vision was years ahead of its time. The first manned spacecraft held only one astronaut and parachuted back to Earth. Although the essence of the idea—a returnable spaceship—was sound, almost thirty years were to pass before it was realised in the Space Shuttle.

The Shuttle stands on its tail on the launch pad. It takes off as a rocket, orbits Earth as a spaceship and re-enters the atmosphere to glide down to a runway like a plane. Its size dwarfs all previous spaceships. Many Mercury capsules would easily fit into its payload bay.

The Shuttle system has three main parts. The most complex is the orbiter. A plane with delta-shaped wings, it has in the tail three large rocket engines that burn liquid hydrogen and liquid oxygen. Two smaller orbital manoeuvring system engines are also present on either side of its vertical tail. These are used for the final push to orbit, for orbit changes and for braking action for return to Earth. An additional 44 small rocket engines are also present in the tail and nose of the orbiter and are used to turn the orbiter in space.

The front end of the orbiter houses the crew on two decks. The upper is the flight deck where up to four crew members sit for launch and re-entry. Below is the mid-deck where three more crew members may sit. The mid-deck serves as the living quarters. It also has a hatch that enables crew members to go out into the payload bay for space walking or to enter ESA's Spacelab when it is on board.

For launch, the orbiter is attached to a large brown external tank. The tank, looking something like a farm silo, carries 1,449,000 liters of liquid hydrogen and 541,000 liters of liquid oxygen (376,000 and 140,000 gal.) for the orbiter's main engines. On the sides of the tank are two solid rocket boosters that provide much of the Shuttle's lift-off thrust. Upright, the Space Shuttle stands 55.7 m (184 ft) tall.

The Space Shuttle *Columbia* being assembled, several months before its first flight on April 12, 1981.

SHUTTLING TO SPACE

A typical Shuttle flight begins in the morning hours at the Kennedy Space Center, Florida. The Shuttle's three main engines are activated at T (take-off) minus four seconds. By the time they throttle to full power, the solid rocket boosters erupt with a brilliant orange flame and huge billowing white clouds. Slowly at first, the Shuttle climbs off the pad and clears the launch tower. Its engines tilt so that their thrust turns the vehicle to aim it for the correct angle for orbit. After just over two minutes of flight, the boosters are exhausted; they separate and return to Earth by parachute to land in the Atlantic Ocean. They can be recovered and reused for future flights.

Climbing now on just the power of its three main engines, the orbiter is almost lying on its back with its belly and the external tank above. High above the ocean, the propellants are finally exhausted and the tank is released and destroyed when it re-enters the atmosphere. The final push for space orbit comes from the small orbital manoeuvring system engines.

More than 160 km (100 mi) up and moving nearly 29,000 km/h (18,000 mph) parallel to Earth's surface, the Shuttle is ready for orbit. The crew inside opens the large payload bay doors. The doors have radiators that help keep the vehicle at the right temperature. On this flight the payload is two communications satellites. On other missions, the payload may be Spacelab or spacecraft destined to travel to another planet. When ready, each satellite is spun to give it a stabilising motion, like a spinning bullet, and is then sprung out of the bay. Later, booster rockets on the satellites direct them to their final orbits. On some missions, broken down and worn out satellites are brought into the bay for repairs by space-suited astronauts.

Space Shuttle *Challenger* lifts off with the Spacelab payload inside.

The Space Shuttle and the cargo bay are clearly visible in this rare shot of the orbiter taken from a nearby satellite.

Another crew member floats down through a hatch to the mid-deck below. There she removes an experiment from a locker and prepares blood samples for testing. Next to her another crew member prepares dinner for the rest of the crew. He pulls prepackaged meals from a locker and adds water to some of the packs. Other packs are inserted into an oven for warming while food packs and utensils are arranged on lap trays. Dinner time can be tricky. Hasty movements with spoons can launch chocolate pudding missiles across the deck. A bump with a fork and a frankfurter will drift away.

When the workday ends, the crew go to bed. Sleeping bags are brought out and crew members climb inside. Some choose to sleep in launch seats while others attach themselves to walls or just float about freely. Right side up or upside down doesn't matter in space.

At the end of the mission, the crew stows all equipment and prepares for re-entry. The orbiter is aimed so that its tail points in the direction it is moving. The orbital manoeuvring system engines fire again, slowing the orbiter so that it falls out of orbit and starts its return. Re-entry starts over the Pacific Ocean. The orbiter, now aimed so that its belly is pointed down, is soon subjected to intense heat from friction with the thin upper atmosphere.

(Left) The flight deck of the orbiter *Discovery* was photographed during final assembly in California before being shipped to the NASA Kennedy Space Center. During flight, the mission commander sits on the left and the pilot on the right. (Above) Crew member Rhea Seddon 'sits' down to a meal in space.

Orbiter *Discovery* glides to a landing after a seven-day flight in space.

THE SMALLEST SPACESHIP

It isn't necessary for a spaceship to have sleek lines like the Space Shuttle. The Apollo lunar module was anything but sleek. Size isn't very important either, providing the spaceship protects the astronaut inside from the dangers of outer space and enables the astronaut to move around. Although the Mercury spaceship was tiny, there is one that is even smaller. It is just large enough for an astronaut to wriggle inside and it comes in two main pieces. One piece has the same shape as the astronaut and goes by the technical name of Extravehicular Mobility Unit, and the other is the Manned Maneuvering Unit (MMU). In simpler words, this is a space suit with a rocket "backpack."

A space suit, when joined to a Manned Maneuvering Unit, becomes a flexible spaceship that enables the astronaut inside to perform a variety of tasks too intricate for the Shuttle to do. On several Shuttle missions astronauts have used this combination to leave the Shuttle's payload bay and bring in broken satellites to repair them or to bring them back to Earth.

The suit portion of this tiny spaceship is remarkable. It has to provide a miniature Earth environment for the astronaut inside while remaining flexible enough for hands, fingers, arms and legs to move easily. The walls of the suit are made of many layers. Pressure is provided by some layers and others provide insulation against temperatures in space that can jump from freezing to frying. An outer layer protects inner layers from impact with tiny meteoroids and from rips.

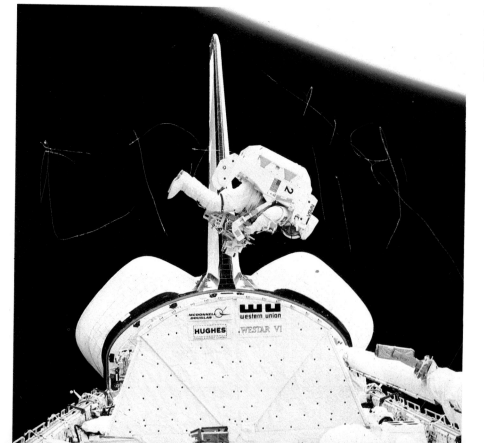

While Bruce McCandless flew about in space with his Manned Maneuvering Unit, a crew member on board the *Challenger* took this picture.

Getting into the suit is something like pulling on trousers and slipping on a sweatshirt. The "doorway" is at the waist and special rings lock the pieces together to make the suit airtight. Gloves are also locked on and a bubble helmet is placed over the head. Oxygen for breathing, cooling water, electric power and radio all come from a life-support system worn on the back. A display and control module that serves as a small control panel for running the suit's systems is worn on the chest.

If the space walker doesn't have to do any complex work outside the payload bay, the walker just clips on to safety lines and moves about the bay using hand holds. However, if work outside the bay is necessary, the MMU is used.

The MMU looks a bit like a white cradle and is mounted to a payload bay wall. The astronaut prepares it for use by opening its arms and turning on its power, then turns around and backs into it. The MMU provides a snug cradle for the life-support system of the space suit. One snap and it is in place, ready to go. Two controls, one for each hand, operate eight clusters of three rocket nozzles. To go forward, the four nozzles pointing straight back are fired. To go up, the ones pointing straight down are fired. To turn around, two nozzles in the front on one side fire, along with two nozzles at the back on the other side.

Rocket fuel that burns would be too dangerous for the astronaut. Instead, the MMU fires compressed nitrogen gas that is held in two high-pressure tanks inside. In this way, the MMU is like a glorified balloon that flies when the air is released.

(Left) Robert Stewart approaches the cabin of the orbiter using the controls of his Manned Manoeuvring Unit.
(Above) Stewart backs away from the orbiter in a fly-around test of the Manned Manoeuvring Unit.

CHALLENGER'S CHALLENGE

On a bright January morning in 1986, the Space Shuttle *Challenger* rose majestically on two brilliant orange pillars of flame. Billowing white smoke trailed upward. Seven astronauts, including one schoolteacher, eagerly anticipated their arrival in orbit and the start of the Shuttle programme's twenty-fifth mission in space. *Challenger*'s engines tilted to steer it towards its proper course. Soon the engines throttled down to 64 percent thrust to reduce vibrations during 'Max Q,' when *Challenger* passes through the sound barrier. At seventy-three seconds mission elapsed time, just moments after return to full throttle, *Challenger* was gone. Unknown to the crew, mission controllers in Houston, or to anyone else, the right solid rocket booster had sprung a leak. Flames from the burning solid rocket fuel shot out like a blowtorch and detonated the propellants in the external tank. In less than one second, *Challenger* was smashed and engulfed in the huge fireball. The solid rocket boosters, now freed from their attachment with the external tank, survived the inferno and streaked off in twisting, unstable flight, leaving spiderlike clouds.

The worst of all fears had come true. With the tragic loss of the *Challenger* the US manned space programme was grounded. A time of world-wide mourning followed for the crew of seven— Francis Scobee, Judith Resnik, Ronald McNair, Michael Smith, Ellison Onizuka, Gregory Jarvis, and teacher Christa McAuliffe.

There were investigations and study commissions and suggestions of what went wrong and recommendations of what needed to be corrected. Though tragic, the loss of the *Challenger* was only a temporary setback in the exploration and use of outer space. Interest in spaceships as a means of reaching space to deploy payloads, conduct experiments and visit space stations has actually increased.

(Left) Fifteen seconds before it exploded, signs of unusual smoke development appeared near the lower end of *Challenger*.
(Below) The detonation of *Challenger*'s external tank shattered the orbiter and permitted the solid rocket boosters to career away.

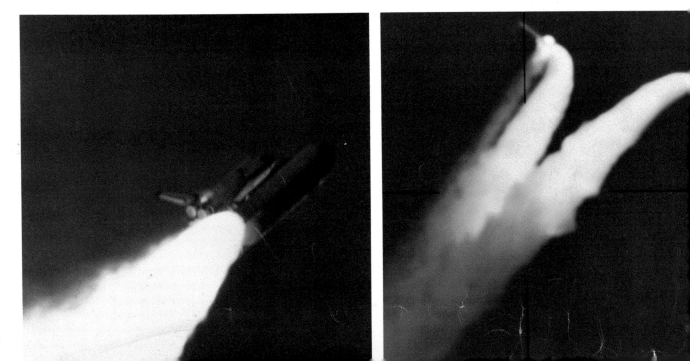

Pieces of the *Challenger* were rescued from the Atlantic Ocean and were returned to Cape Canaveral for evaluation.

A replacement Shuttle for the *Challenger* is under construction. Improvements have been made in safety procedures and equipment, and intensive retraining has been given to staff members. The Shuttle orbiter *Discovery* went into space in September 1988. While NASA rebuilds its Shuttle fleet, the organisation is making extensive plans for putting a permanent space station in orbit in the 1990s. At the same time, a second generation, low-cost shuttle is being studied that would fill the gap between the Space Shuttles, when they retire, and the National Aerospace Plane, which, it is hoped, will begin service early in the twenty-first century.

The tragedy of the *Challenger* has done little to dampen enthusiasm for manned space flight or for shuttle-like vehicles. The Soviet Union has built and flown a Space Shuttle of its own and the European Space Agency is constructing one. Japan's space agency is planning a Hermes-class shuttle it calls the *Hope*, and has made wind tunnel and gliding drop tests of models of it. The United Kingdom is planning an aerospace plane and West Germany has proposed a shuttle vehicle with both the first and second stages capable of runway landings.

The Space Shuttle *Discovery*, without its main engines, is worked on at the Kennedy Space Center.

HERMES, THE SPACE PLANE

The French space agency, called the Centre National d'Etudes Spatiales or CNES, has been studying the concept of a spaceplane since 1976. It will be Europe's entry to manned space flight. Called Hermes, the vehicle will be half the Shuttle's size and have about a quarter of its payload capacity. If successful, it will provide a less expensive alternative to the Space Shuttle when only a small payload and crew are needed in orbit.

CNES decided to follow the Shuttle's example rather than the Apollo or Soyuz space capsules because it has greater versatility in returning to Earth. Both Apollo and Soyuz have limited control during re-entry into the atmosphere and the acceleration forces experienced by the crew are considerable. As a spaceplane, the Hermes has much greater manoeuvrability, and because it makes a horizontal runway landing like the Shuttle, it makes a more comfortable ride for the crew.

Hermes looks like a small Space Shuttle. It has a bullet-shaped body 18 m (59 ft) long and triangular wings 10 m (33 ft) wide. It has two vertical tails that give it additional stability when gliding back to Earth. The payload bay has doors that open like the Shuttle's, and inside is space for 35 cu m (45.8 cu yd) of cargo.

Hermes, standing on its tail, will be launched by Ariane-5. This rocket, yet to be built, will be a versatile booster that can also be used for unmanned payloads such as satellites. It will look something like the Shuttle's solid rocket boosters and external tank. Two solid fuel boosters will flank a large rocket that uses liquid hydrogen and liquid oxygen. Together, the three rockets will produce enough thrust to raise the 17-metric-ton Hermes into low orbit.

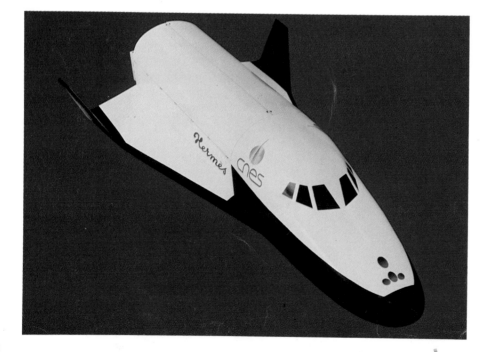

The European Space Agency's proposed manned spaceplane, Hermes, will be able to carry small crews and payloads economically to space and then fly back to Earth for a runway landing.

The cargo bay of Hermes carries a satellite and a Spacelab pallet mounted with experiments. Two astronauts, wearing space suits, prepare the payload for deployment.

Hermes is shown as it would look in orbit. A mechanical arm helps space-walking astronauts handle the payload.

A typical mission for Hermes will begin at the European Space Agency's Kourou launch site in French Guiana in South America, where Ariane rockets are presently launched. Up to six crew members will climb aboard and rocket into space on the power of the two solid-fuel and one liquid-fuel engines. After separation, Hermes will push itself into orbit on the thrust of two medium-sized engines located in its tail. Smaller engines, mounted at various locations, will steer the spaceplane.

On some missions, Hermes will deploy payloads, but on others it will rendezvous with the planned American space station. Europe is building a portion of the station named the Columbus. Hermes will dock with Columbus for as long as 90 days before returning to Earth. In this way, the new spaceplane will serve as a space station shuttle craft.

Following its stay in space, the engines in the Hermes tail will fire again, slowing it down so that it can begin its long glide to Earth. A reusable heat shield system will protect it from the searing friction with the atmosphere. The mission will come to an end as Hermes' wheels touch the runway in Kourou or in Istres in France. It will then be made ready for another mission.

When someone has a good idea, it's not long before others follow. NASA has the Space Shuttle and ESA is developing Hermes. The Soviet Union has built its own shuttle, the *Buran*.

The *Buran* is in some ways a copy of the United States Space Shuttle. *Buran* is the same size and shape as a Space Shuttle orbiter, and even has a payload bay in its back, too. *Buran* operates in space and glides to a runway like the Space Shuttle does. One big difference is the way *Buran* is launched. It has a liquid propellant core vehicle, called the Energia, that looks like a Shuttle external tank but has rocket engines at its base. (The Shuttle external tank has no engines of its own.) Strapped to the outside of the Energia are four liquid propellant booster rockets. Following launch, the boosters are returned to Earth by parachute but the Energia is destroyed. Another difference is that the *Buran* can fly in space totally unmanned. On its first flight in November 1988, there was no crew on board!

Shuttles that stand on their tails for launch aren't the only entries into the reusable space vehicle business. A British company is looking at the development of a HOTOL vehicle. The odd-sounding name stands for 'horizontal take-off and landing' · The HOTOL is a hybrid vehicle that combines the best features of jet planes with those of the Space Shuttle.

Jet planes take off on horizontal runways. Fuel is carried in tanks built inside the plane's wings. Jets don't have to carry oxygen because their engines suck in air to mix with the fuel so that it can burn. This makes jet planes very efficient when compared with the Space Shuttle. The Shuttle has to carry oxygen as well as fuel so that its engines can work in the vacuum of space.

An artist's drawing of one version of the National Aerospace Plane. Slots located on the underside are air intakes for the hybrid engines.

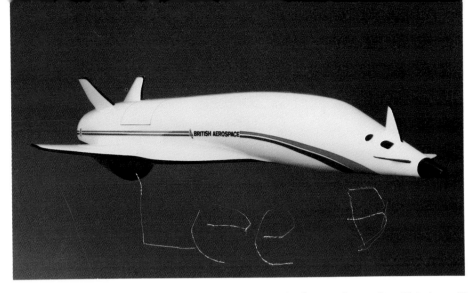

The United Kingdom's aerospace plane, HOTOL, is intended to begin service first as an unmanned payload launcher and later to carry crew and passengers.

HOTOL's engines will suck in air like a jet's engines. It will take off on an airport runway. However, when it reaches an altitude where there is too little air for the engines to operate, the engines will convert to rockets and drain oxygen from a liquid oxygen tank. After reaching orbit, it will return to Earth as a plane and restart its engines for final landing approach.

The HOTOL concept is also being considered by the United States. Scientists refer to it as 'aerospace plane' and look upon it in the future as a less costly way of reaching orbit than the Space Shuttle. Because it may also be used as a passenger vehicle for flights to the Far East, it has been nicknamed the 'Orient Express'. Taking off with a load of passengers at Dulles International Airport outside of Washington, D.C., it will climb quickly in a suborbital path to an altitude of more than 30,480 m (100,000 ft), reaching a top speed of more than 12,880 km/h (8,000 mph), and land in Tokyo, Japan, after only 90 minutes!

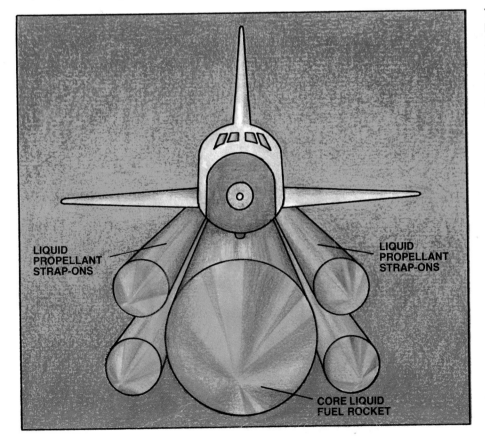

LIQUID PROPELLANT STRAP-ONS

LIQUID PROPELLANT STRAP-ONS

CORE LIQUID FUEL ROCKET

The largest of two shuttles being developed by the Soviet Union resembles NASA's Space Shuttle, except that it has four boosters surrounding the external tank.

FUTURE SPACESHIPS

Science fiction often gives us glimpses of the future. Many science fiction writers have invented fantastic spaceships capable of crossing the Universe at the speed of light. Although words like 'warp drive' or 'hyperdrive' are often used, little explanation is given about how they work. Though someday we *may* be able to travel at light speeds or beyond, for the foreseeable future we will have to be content with spaceships driven by conventional power plants. Most will use chemical rocket engines that produce thrust by burning chemical propellants. However, there are some interesting alternatives that actually work or seem feasible.

In the 1960s, NASA began research on a rocket engine called the ion drive. Though electrically operated, it uses the same action-reaction principle of chemical rockets. The idea is simple. An ion engine is about the size of a small wastepaper basket. A supply of mercury is slowly converted to an electrified gas similar to that found inside fluorescent lights. The atoms of mercury in the gas are electrically charged and are called 'ions'. They are attracted and repelled by magnets.

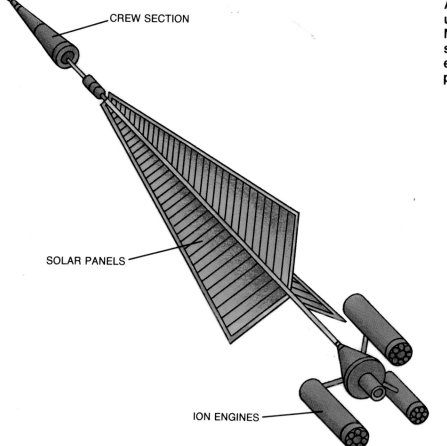

CREW SECTION

SOLAR PANELS

ION ENGINES

An ion drive rocket could be used for manned flights to Mars. The panels contain solar cells for making electricity from sunlight to power the engines.

IMPORTANT SPACESHIP DATES

12 April 1961 Yuri Gagarin becomes the first human to enter space and orbit Earth.

5 May 1961 Alan Shepard becomes the first American to enter space.

20 February 1962 John Glenn becomes the first American to orbit Earth.

16 July 1969 *Apollo 11*, the first manned mission to land on the Moon, is launched.

15 July 1975 The American and Soviet Apollo-Soyuz linkup in space begins.

12 April 1981 The Space Shuttle *Columbia* makes its first flight into space.

7 February 1984 Bruce McCandless test flies the Manned Manoeuvring Unit during a space walk outside the Space Shuttle.

28 January 1986 The Space Shuttle *Challenger* and its crew of seven are destroyed in a launch explosion.

29 September 1988 The Space Shuttle *Discovery* is launched into space.

15 November 1988 The Soviet Space Shuttle *Buran* makes its first flight into space.

The engine produces an electromagnetic field that shoots the ions out of the back of the engine to provide thrust. Engines like these have been used in space tests with great success. Their thrust is very low when compared with chemical engines, but they can operate for months at a time building up the spaceship's speed until it is travelling many times faster than one using chemical rockets. Someday, when manned spaceflights to Jupiter and beyond become possible, ion engines may provide the necessary power.

A variation of the ion-drive principle has been tested so far only on Earth. This propulsion system is called the mass driver. A heavy object such as a rock is placed in a magnetic bucket on a track and accelerated to high speed by an electromagnetic field. At the end of the track, the bucket stops and throws out its rock payload. The result is a strong action/reaction force. A continuous stream of rocks thrown by such a system could propel a spaceship. The problem is to find enough rocks. One solution may be to capture a small asteroid and chip it into pieces for the propellant. Whether or not anyone would like to go to all this trouble is another matter.

A third possibility for future spaceship propulsion is the use of a solar sail concept. This idea was seriously considered for an American space-probe encounter with Halley's Comet. The Sun produces a tremendous amount of energy that is released into space. One form of this energy is a stream of high-speed charged particles known as the solar wind. The idea of the solar sail is to erect a very large sail of thin material to capture solar wind and use it to sail through the Solar System pulling a spaceship. The idea has yet to be tested, but in theory, a sail about 0.65 sq km (0.5 sq mi) in size should be enough to drag a spacecraft to an encounter with a comet.

Space shuttles, solar sails, mass and ion drivers offer good possibilities for our future in space. The new spaceships planned and being built promise to bring a time when travel through space will be just as common as commercial airline travel is today.

(Above) NASA's design for a 700 sq m (840 sq yd) solar sail of very thin aluminised plastic. It was intended to capture the solar wind and sail out with a payload of instruments to meet Halley's Comet. The mission was never funded. **(Left)** A more advanced solar sail concept involves many 'spokes' of thin plastic material extending from the hub of instruments by as much as 7.4 km (4.5 mi). The sail would spin like a helicopter rotor as it travelled through the Solar System.

GLOSSARY

Action Reaction Scientific principle which states that for every action (rocket thrust) there is an opposite and equal reaction (rocket movement)

Apollo Project name given to the three-astronaut space capsule used for the American trips to the Moon, the Skylab programme and the **Apollo-Soyuz** flight (American and Soviet)

Ariane Family of rockets used by the European Space Agency to launch satellites into orbit

Astronaut American name for someone who flies through space

Aerospace plane Proposed plane/rocket that will economically transport payloads into low Earth orbit and carry passengers around the world at high speed

Atlas An American unmanned satellite launching rocket

Buran The Soviet Space Shuttle

Centre National d' Etudes Spatiales (CNES) The French space agency

Command module The space capsule part of Apollo

Cosmonaut Russian name for someone who flies through space

Delta An American unmanned satellite launching rocket

European Space Agency (ESA)–An organisation of ten European nations working together on space research

External tank Giant liquid fuel tank for the Space Shuttle

Gemini Project name for the American two-astronaut space capsule used for Earth orbital flights

Hermes The proposed French shuttle-type manned space vehicle to be launched by Ariane-5

Hope The Japanese Hermes-class shuttle

HOTOL Horizontal Take-off and Landing vehicle proposed by the United Kingdom for economical Earth-to-orbit transportation

Ion Drive Rocket propulsion system that magnetically expels electrically charged particles out of the engine to provide thrust

Light year The distance light travels in one year (about 9.7 million million km or 6 million million mi)

Lunar Module The Moon landing vehicle used by Apollo astronauts

Manned Manoeuvring Unit (MMU) Rocket backpack unit worn by astronauts for moving around outside the Space Shuttle

Mercury Project name given to the American one-astronaut Earth orbital and suborbital space flights

Orbiter Plane/rocket/space capsule portion of the Space Shuttle

Saturn V Giant American rocket used to launch the Apollo Moon flights and the Skylab space station

Service module Section attached to the Apollo command module, that provides rocket thrust, oxygen and electrical power

Solar sail A proposed thin film space vehicle that moves through space by capturing the high-speed particles ejected by the Sun (solar wind)

Solar wind Particles ejected into space by the Sun

Solid rocket booster (SRB) Solid-fuel booster rockets attached to the external tank of the Space Shuttle

Spacelab A scientific laboratory built by the European Space Agency that fits inside the payload bay of the Space Shuttle

Sputnik Russian word for satellite

Soyuz Soviet two-cosmonaut space capsule currently in use for Earth orbital missions

Titan An American unmanned satellite-launching rocket

V2 German rocket used for launching bombs during World War II

Voskhod Soviet three-cosmonaut space capsule for Earth orbital missions

INDEX